MW00913162

INSTANCE PRESS

Another Instance: Three Chapbooks
© Jack Collom, Camille Guthrie, Mark McMorris 2011

ISBN: 978-0-9679854-9-7

Book design & typesetting: Good Utopian
Set in Jenson with News Gothic titles

Library of Congress Control Number: 2011933622

Instance Press books are available from Small Press Distribution
1341 Seventh Street, Berkeley, CA 94710
1-800-869-7533
www.spdbooks.org
www.instancepress.com

ANOTHER **INSTANCE**

THREE CHAPBOOKS

JACK COLLOM

CAMILLE GUTHRIE

MARK McMORRIS

JACK COLLOM
Lumping & Splitting

for Marcella Durand and Jonathan Skinner

☆ re-do?

& SPLITTING

LIMPING

Jack
Collom

FRONTISPIECE

There was a beast (we can be sure
                    of that)
Went lumping through the woods
                    looking for food.
S/he pawed both berries and bodies,
                    splitting fat
From lean and sweet from mean,
        according to mood.

Along with food came figments. Each contained
Confounded glues and incongruities.
All babbled but roughcut cut
                    into Named
Entities. The second (that) foot fell,
                    Linnaeus

Left home. & instamatic
                    impressionism,
It formed a sort of farm; the
                    image danced
Within its skin —— good for pragmatism,
Tender... (long woods by the way).
        Eventually writing chanced

Its way onto some scum, pressed,
                    clumsy,
Rebuilding visions: skritch-scratch,
        whams and whimsy.

LUMPING & SPLITTING
A personal essay that breaks down into a poem, etc.

—to all snowflakes

"... exactly like a tree!"
                              --Gulliver

There are bumps on bumps on bumps on bumps on bumps on bumps on bumps on bumps on bumps.

Suppertimes, when I was a boy, I used to eat my mashed potatoes, and green beans, and baloney, and drink my milk, with a definite emphasis on dividing the different foods and savoring them separately. I knew, of course, that the different foods would get totally scrambled in my tummy, but I was intent on individuation so long as the tastebuds (lump with other senses) were involved. Sure, I put salt on my potatoes, and I went much further than "putting on" when it came to gravy: I'd shape the mashed into a nice heap and carefully excavate "mines" into its mass. I'd load these mines with brown gravy, seal 'em up, and then go in and "discover" rich copper lodes. Delicious! I split the lumps.

But I didn't, for example, combine a bite of simple meat with a string-bean.

Meanwhile, my parents were sitting there in the form of great, judgmental, silent bears, staring at me. Not really. They were eating and talking and passing things on request.

My thinking in those years was lumpy too: adolescent metaphysics.*

Later I did come to appreciate the glories of mixture, sometimes to extremes. I think my life's been a mix of those nonmix Illinois days (of vegetables // meat; body // mind; woods // language; etc.) with mixy immersions. Fear and delight having sex in the stomach.
                    * * * (*)

In ornithology, some of the people interested in classification are classified as either lumpers or splitters; they mentally sort wild birds

* Though the texture often resembled a purée.

Let's
Unclog
Mandatory
Precision.

Light
Undermines
Mental
Preparedness.

Loosen
Up,
M'sieu
Picky-pick!

Listen!
Upper air's
Malleable
Philosophy...

So,
Put
Light
Into
Truth?

Suchness
Perpetuates
Likeness
If
Twinned.

Somehow
Play
Limbers
It all up
Tastefully.

Sort
Particulars.
Lock.
Impeach
Time.

either by grouping somewhat disparate kinds of birds into one species (lumpers) or by dividing even slight variations into separate species categories (splitters). For example, the Bullock's oriole, a western bird, has been lumped together with the Baltimore oriole of the east, though their plumages are clearly different (you can tell them apart as far as you can distinguish a dressed-up woman from a bearded man, but then feathers aren't even skin-deep either), into the new, and blandly made, "northern oriole" nomenclature, chiefly because the two orioles, where their ranges overlap, do often inter-breed. (One couldn't suspect orioles of bestiality for Christ's sake; thus they must be conspecific.)

Similarly, Audubon's and myrtle warblers are now just yellow-rumped warblers, as if the myrtle's elegant white chin were naught. There are many, many examples of lumping, some of splitting, and the classification of avifauna never reaches, probably never will reach, perfect stasis. The proverbial (panverbal) tides move back and forth, and wayward eddies develop as well. (Thus time itself goes to the splitters.)

LOOK OUT, KING GEORGE, A TINY (MASSIVE, AVERAGE) MEMBER OF THE WORLDWIDE BACTERIA CONSORTIUM IS ENTERING YOUR LEFT VENTRICLE!

Do you like to think (deep breath) "SKY!" or divide it, like the irregular grid of a winter deciduous tree (unintentionally?) does, into aesthetic geometries, or perhaps divide it into its own ripples and greenish shadings? Or make other atmospheric distinctions, clear down to the sky-continuous inside your clothes? Or what? Do you like life or ice cream or Ben 'n' Jerry's chocolate fudge (or TCBY)? We know enough by now to abolish binaries, and then haul them halfway back.

(1)   I find that my ornithological sentiments are with the splitters. I feel an almost personal affront at the Bullock's being so broadly categorized, having its glittering identity smeared, as it were.... (Though the name "Bullock's" sounds like a nasty smear itself.) There's a way in which birders tend to see a bird species as tantamount to an individual person; we identify/personify the species (chickadees are unbelieveably perky, endearing, and secretly cruel") and seldom the individual within it (though many exceptions there) a la T. W. Burgess's Reddy the Fox (all foxes) and Sammy Jay (all blue jays). Perhaps, conversely, each person sees himherself (context: part of the supraspecies human ((we think)) world) as a species;

3

clearly each poet can be seen as a taxonomic entity, each dictator as a painfully particularized type.

PSYCHIC GEOMETRY OF PRECEDING PARAGRAPH (1)

re birds, like tangent, not overlap
but love overlap
but/and value backwash
but lump in order to split
always seed of the opposite lies within
I cop to place in scale
switch to different particulars when scale expands

YELLOWS

Kasimir Malevich sat up and stretched his arms as high as he could reach, closing both his eyes hard. Then he arose, stumbled down the narrow hall and peed, dark yellow into a pale yellow toilet bowl. He called downstairs, "Good morning, wife! Are you perhaps making scrambled eggs?"

"No!" she answered, "I'm planning the disposition of explosives for an attempted coup, along the Great Boulevard!"

"Then I will cook my own," called Kasimir. He went downstairs; however, he did not cook. He stuffed dry oats in his mouth and began to paint feverishly on a canvas set up in the pantry.

It all came together -- and began to blast apart. Kasimir put everything behind him but only went one-thousandth of a second into the future.

"It's a masterpiece," said Anna Maryova. Then she pushed the button.

(2) I. Anyway, my bird sentiments are with the splitters. I think it's love (which is always selfish on some level) that makes me discriminatory. Love shuns the categorical ((thus we can't stand Ourbelovedselves being categorized).

> PG I.
>
> re birds, like tangent, not overlap
> love overlaps self
> love arrow strikes bull's-eye (species)
> minus name

A. But in and through other aspects of seeing the world and of thinking per se, I'm more of a lumper: like to zoom to the perspective of the big picture when I consider Evolution*, Psychology, Ecology, History, etc.

> PG A.
>
> re world: ♥ lump
> motion, breath
> circles (macro-micro, etc.)

1. My knowledge of birds is more detailed than my knowledge of Evolution; thus the pull to examine in small; thus also the pull to examine Evolution's larger configurations relationally (which entails, just as precisely but with less emphasis on rigidity, BIG details).

> PG 1.
>
> redux
> size ≠ generality
> circle (brain) radiates layering (thought-fields)

a. Plus, I have faith in the coal-and-fire face of the Black-burnian warbler because it's part of a system. A system wherein mutations have been both lumped and worn away, like a forest fire spread over geologic time (burning up sunshine, I guess).

* "chaos with feedback"

PG *(a.)*

+ ↑ (gobble) image, INC.
up & down
input outwits entropy + false homogeneity,
        bogus linearity

i. Just as much (more? in a major/minor way?) I love the
random arrival: jerking metonymy out of its (metonymy's)
poor paltry logic and into the great Whatever.*

                            PG

                            ∴ + ♡ ?
                            various neighbors
                            ? = yes

        (.) Macro and micro have great sex together (sliding
        scales), e.g., lump & split.

                                            PG

                                            growth/1

Skinny little curlyhead, thick lips, epicanthic folds over blue eyes,
unbrushed teeth, age six standing knee-deep in cold poolwater off Lake
Onekama, wherein Daddy had just tossed a bright copper penny (and then
walked away); the penny gleamed at such depth I'd have to immerse my face
in frigid sparkling water to get it. He'd said, "If you can take it, you
can keep it." Standing there. All morning long (in memory). Never got
up the nerve to do it. If I had that cent (with interest) now....
        Same year, same summer stay (lucky) in Uncle Happy's cottage, I
wandered toward the big Lake Michigan beach, came upon that famous eagle
eyrie in a low pine on a dune. Climbed up and even around onto the thick
old nest (it had been bulked up for years—old living messes covered up)
and into it, among the detritus of the just-passed spring's living. Bones
and dried excreta and other mega-raptor garbage. And then down.
        Guess I was chicken about water but a bear for air.

Quoarth strode the darkened alleys
relentlessly, his face a grotesque mask
of unshakeable purpose bedizened with
incidental shadowplay.

Around him the careless city swelled
and shriveled like some grimy heart.
But little by little, the air grew
cleaner, more flecked with light, even
a touch of innocent frolic, as Quoarth,
like a powerful larva, pushed on through
the urban margins.

He laughed.

Analysis & synthesis. Isis's anal sin thesis?
Shall we lump shapelessness with a fork? What
would it lead to? Lump wood with led? It to?
What? I'd lump a hump with a split nit. And a
hot dog with a volcano. And then I'd split.

Jim wrote a story so he'd have something to read. The story began,
"Gustafson scratched his chin! 'This dame was tougher than shoeleather.'"
Then he scratched that out and started again: "The puny Cretaceous
mammal chuckled. The air was getting bad, but it knew where to hide."
His assistant, Emerald, began laughing. "It'll never fly!" she
exclaimed.
He lay in bed, alone, and stared at the walls. They were moving,
yes, but not at a rate with which he was in touch.
Emerald made a mental note to buy some rat poison.
Jim had always wanted to talk to Emerald. Just talk. But somebody
was throwing pebbles at the window. He had to go take care of it.
Two pigeons were billing and cooing on the roof. Ha.

Surprise, relationship between humor and.

See p. 11.

Humor _is_ surprise.

And poetry _is_ surprise.

Therefore - humor _is_ poetry. Well, maybe not quite,

in the sense that Nature is everything, & truth is everything, thus

Nature is truth. But is Truth nature?

Is All everything?

OK, what is humor really?
To answer this, we refer you to The Big Bang.

OK, Big, what's it all about?
Well, there I was, just a smoothness, y'know.
Kinda milky — no, momentary & transparent, like pre-poetic.
And, I don't know, the tiniest variation crept in.
I say "crept" and already we picture a mouse or something.
But y'know if I was a moment, then I couldn't be a moment forever,
    right?
So the littlest thing in the world happened,
let's put it that way. And of course all hell broke loose.
Slowly.

One thing leads to another.
And how can you avoid "one thing"?
If there were really Nothing ... nothing would have happened.
But there was something. Hence everything.

Etc. Well, what's this got to do w/ Surprise? Everything.
Now that we have Anything, as a partially realized condition,
I mean,
         world. Ball mechanics. (Whirled)
Suddenly, language scrawls a partial realization. Which
microcosms along, like a typo for GraCe (like, you know) -
    It kinda looks like a mercury grid on
    mind.
Anyway, it's quasi-linear & quasi-everywhichaway & it functions by
    pushing expectations before it like a snowplow.

As these things pile up exponentially, contraries weasel in constantly.

What else? If the zigzag of same is more or less carnivalesque, i.e.,

    not bad, then — isn't it interesting how "in time" resembles "intime"?

    (margin release for the question mark; what does that tellya?))

Is everybody happy?

WHAT'S the question?

OK, back to work.

③ 　　Think Evolution. Don't you find "change" floating on your mind? And, skintight, "Natural Selection" or "Survival of the Fittest" activating it (change) like underwater paddles? You may then think "variation," or you may assume variation. (All this presumes you don't toss the whole idea into the sea as godless trash.) LONG NECK - MOST SUN-SOAKED LEAVES (YUM) - STRONG! - PLENTY BABIES /// SHORT NECK - O MEDIOCRE GIANT - (DIES UNWED - GENES WITHER).

PG ③

≠
≠/E (pressure)　　　　　　　　　　curlicue
x ≠ y　　　　　　　or　　　　　　erasure
(x ≠ y)　　　　　　　　　　　　"freeze"
((∅))　　　　　　　　　　　　forced regularity
---◁↑∴ —↓0

* see next p. (wherever)

5

④ 　　But, splitting paragraphs, lumpety-lump, "that" (mechanism) is merely Evolution's Dramatic Sensation: THE BATTLE FOR LIFE. Foregrounding The Battle oversimplifies the action. The Battle, despite its turbulence, is static. Ramifying a blockbuster movie or two or three out of it anoints the defineable per se with heroic (cut) laurel (for killing off Ambiguity), utilizes the principle (pineapple?) of variation only as a ladder to a Goal (such as "At last! The Big Brain! Comin' down them Rock Island tracks!")

PG ④

¶ 1:
—◁= ▓▓ = .
blowing up stillness like a balloon...
　　　　pops
walks all over (x ≠ y)
　- e.g. ●← ∧
infinite change　　　　　　　　　(brain)
　　　order born of disorder

re-do

* * * *

We've "always" had techno-battles with the abundant fox squirrels around the house, in regard to our bird feeders. (These were the black oil sunflower seed days, before we switched to the more expensive but squirrel-yucky safflower.) baffles and cunning placements were circumvented by daring leaps and clever climbing routes, if not outright vandalism. The alternating oneupmanship of these struggles resembled competitions between the pre-Socratic Athenians and Darius's Persians.

Our most heroic, fondly-remembered foe was a small female we called Maeve.* She had a raggedy patch of fur on her side but seemed otherwise trim and neat. And she was the Einstein of fox squirrels. She questioned every assumption.

Jenny was sitting bare-legged in the back garden eating an ice cream cone when she felt a scratching at her calf. She looked down and there wiggled a pretty but importunate little squirrel demanding a share. Maeve.

My workroom is a slice of porch wedged between kitchen and garden. Unbroken stretch of windows east and south, great greenleaf vistas. Outside one window hangs a feeder (abandoned now), then frequented mostly by house finches. Squirrels would scoot along the very narrow sill and look up longingly at the seed-laden plastic cylinder just a little too high above their heads. I was treated to many an intense underchin view - only a foot away from me - as they stretched and calculated. Some tried the leap... and clattered to the ground.

But Maeve was lithe, and actually able to spring, grab, hang on and feast. There were complications too tedious to explicate involving nearby vines as well, but the main upshot was I cut a slat of plywood and nailed it to the sill below the feeder - slanting between window and sill - to foil Maeve's leaping forays.

Then the brave and dogged creature began to eat the plywood, to regain her flat launching pad, and... perhaps the wood was toxic... perhaps some sly neighborhood cat... Maeve disappeared.

We were bereft.

No other squirrel since her day has come close.

She was a lumper and a splitter.

---

* After the great goddess-queen of Connacht, in Irish lore. Her name is also written "Medb" and means "she who intoxicates." She mated with at least nine mortal kings and dominated them all. She was a shape-shifter; if you see a withered hag guarding a well, it might be Maeve. The story goes that once the famous warrior Cú Chulainn hounded and slew the squirrel riding on Maeve's shoulder, thereby causing her to lose an important battle. Later she devised the demise of Cú Chulainn: the enchanted Children of Cailatin lured him to his death, fighting the entire force of Ireland. Maeve at last was killed by a vengeful nephew using a slingshot and a lump of hard cheese.

* * When Cú Chulainn goes berserk or into "warp spasm,"
his body revolves within its skin,
his hair stands out from his head,
one eye sinks into his head while the other bulges out onto his cheek,
his muscles swell to enormous size,
and a hero light rises from his head.
He gives a giant howl and all the local spirits howl with him.
In these fits, he cannot distinguish between friend and foe.

(5)   The real cool, hot, down-'n'-dirty sensation of Evolution "is"**
Variation itself. Can you picture a totally homogeneous Universe? What
exact texture? Now that we know about scales, can you picture a micro
without a ... wave? A macro without a biota? Given the tiniest Difference,
anywhere: the whole thing is (maybe) Off & Running !?!?!?!? & % () : Which means
Mutations. Are basic, and not monstrous. Which means mutations are basic
and not monstrous. Which means mutations aRe basic and not monstrous.
Which means mutations must be everywhere. Not only life's composed of
them, but S-P-A-C-E it"Self." And of course Time. (And the course it
rolled in on...) Not only is time a tissue of mutations at any given frozen
instant, anywhere (now picture "anywhere"), but homogeneity exists at ALL _only_
(echo echo) as an Ideal (think about it, 1, 1, 1) one two three. "Zooming
to the Big Picture" (Evol.) can be an avenue, a ramification, to at least
a principle of Chaos. Breath is to hurricane as zoom is to WHAT? Wm.
Jennings Bryan had it backwards. Natural Selection is just the politics
of Nature. In this light, Context is light.

from
pages
back * Extinct math ideas (unlike old theories in physics) can come to life again
        at any point. Because pure truth is unpredictable.

** Whatta word!

To write a sonnet as an early morning
Exercise. Along with stretches, lifts,
And feed the parakeet. Without fair warning,
Plunge--then see if pool - or empty rifts -

Might greet my pen. Oh well. One easy out
Presents itself: I hear the finches chirping
In the garden. Whip this up. No doubt
A happy froth can "write itself," and burping

With contentment, I can then proceed
Along the "beefsteak" of the day fullspeed.
I mean consumption, quenching every need,
Homogenization--I am Satan's weed!

As such, I think I've earned your frank respect;
Within myself, I bleed (breed) Excess and conflict!

Once upon a time there was a piece of cardboard named Carl. He was
in love with another piece of cardboard named Misty. But they both lay
there separate and lonesome until their friend Elmer brought them together,
and they lived happily ever after.
Especially Elmer.

Marble slab encrusted with lichens: a primitive plant community.

A couple nights ago we fell into the TV and found "The Uninvited" (1944). I saw this film when I was twelve, and a moment in it has remained my sharpest cinematic memory: when Ray Milland and Gail Russell, already ghost-addled nearly to hysteria by some very pushy spooks, are feverishly discussing things and the large double door behind them BURSTS open—exploding the word "sudden" to a new extreme—but silently. Memory had translated this moment to a SLAM for me; perhaps some inner daydream-editor didn't trust silence to be such a Shock.

My crush on shy, ebony-haired Gail Russell was foiled (or deliciously darkened) by her early death from alcoholism.

PG (5)   "long way from home"

Evol * = (x ≠ y)
does "to see" = (x ≠ y)?
can "exact" = 0?
◀ · w/o *uuu*?   (a particle)
◀ universe w/o motion?
fitting of opposites complicates gravity

every little bit helps,
step-by-step,
generate,
what's "the" big IDEA?
space drags time & vice versa
any ≠ ⊞   (picture)
thought's repetition, via vowels
on the road(s) again
?s at the end of the tunnel
one, two = infinity, ?   (comma ≈ "is to")
(branch)   ——◀ = HEY HEY HEY HEY HEY
insulighghght

SPLITLUMP

Can you tell them apart?
Does each prepare for the other?
Are they like "names"?
Do they divert attention from each squirming ontology?
Do they resemble tools—axes and glue—too procedural?
Is every circle a spiral?
Is every line a ladder?
Are they words? "Lump," "split"?
Is writing flat?
Does boustrophedon imply two dimensions?
Does an open mouth imply three?

And the spiritual lumping that's indeed going on,

PG

yes

in a contrary partnership

yes yes

with the pragmatic splitting active in the Law of the Jungle,

what the hell

is Symbiosis. Living on a ball,
the armcurve of the symbiont far outweighs the angular clash (withal very
real) of the rival.

symbiosis, then selection

$$O , \curvearrowright > \lightning$$

From the mitochondria (slightly alien "artists-in-residence"-cum-energy-
mavens within each cell) to the intricate cybernetic loops of evaporating,
condensing worldwide water,

$$\star \rightarrow \partial \wp = yes$$

the fact is: Things Work Together.

(note ingredients)

// That variety of working together called Friction (Friendship, Strife,
Boxing, Divorce, War)

spotlight on $\lightning$

is more on our two-leg, five-foot scale, so it gets the headlines
(UEBERMART DRIVES HANK'S DRUGS BANKRUPT), but there's the rub,

the passing warmth

the incidental warmth within the entropy of any paradigm... // Death.

0

fluid finds a way

INDEX I — Fractal: The dimension situation in the instant of pinching up a tablecloth.

INDEX II — Ich weiss dass ich nichts weiss.

INDEX III — see SURFACES.

INDEX IV — What is haziness? Help!

INDEX V — Lumping displays splitting, which displays lumping.

INDEX VI — Ask Leibniz for a glass of water.

INDEX VII — "The incomprehensible bustle of life" (Mahler), quoted in many fonts, exhaled in a cloud of smoke.

INDEX VIII — Mathematical complexity includes the imaginary.

INDEX IX — Walking in a <u>different</u> balance of nature, the Second Law of Thermodynamics is a growing boy.

INDEX XXXXXXXXX — "The classification of the constituents of a chaos, nothing less is here essayed." (Melville in <u>Moby-Dick</u>)

INDEX 11 — Not that I don't love little things and feel that both God and the Devil are in the details; I believe most people err by both generalizing the detail and failing to even swim out to the big picture. When I err (constantly) I try to do it in my own specific (albeit dichotomous) way. The man who got me started in birding, Sam Keen (when we were both 11), recently taught me an eye exercise wherein one holds one's thumbs at least a foot apart, both thumbs in line with the eyes, and shifts focus back and forth between them, seeing a whole thumb and a pair of translucent thumbs at each switch.

INDEX finger — Closure and "the like," Partliness, degrees of chaos, deconstructing deconstruction, irrational numbers... "uncertainty theory," gestural indeterminacy, spirals of sunflowers & galaxies, secondary functions, St. Narcissus, So Bad It's Good, gender politics, identity problemz, motion as imperfection, revolving evolution, logorrhea's economy, primitive song, sadomasochism, watering the plants, multiple intelligences, flapping and gliding, in and out (utter wordlessness), falsetto, bone and face paper ground glossolalia dry humor a walk in the woods the dancing spectator light filler light filler dream outwitting the censor and hay golpes en la vida, tan fuertes . . . Yo no sé! let's eat...

INDEX 12 —   ON MARGINS

   In an excellent article (in <u>Natural History</u>, Sept. '02), Menno
Schilthuizen discusses hybrids in various aspects (including the proud
nugget that "hybrid" has the same root as "hubris" — hybrids were thought
to be "arrogance or insolence against the gods"). Crosses are more
important than previously realized in providing variations for evolution
to work on; like mutations they bring about interesting new genetic
arrangements, which may or may not, then, "work."

   Schilthuizen describes "hybrid zones," where any two interbreeding
species overlap. Paradoxically, the center of a hybrid zone tends to be
relatively barren of hybrids — likewise of the basic species. This is
due to concentrations of the potential for weakness - genetic defects -
wreaking havoc with the population. One could look upon the hybrid zone
as a large marginal area, so large that it has margins of its own. It is
in the margins <u>of</u> the margins that the lively proliferations take place;
there's something salubrious about a minority situation - it works like
a spice.

   One might compare, then, the situation of postmodern literature,
the initial rationale for which was to hybridize, and thus increase the
possibilities of, modern literature, which had become too pure and insolent
a strain (liable perhaps to aesthetic inbreeding). But as the (literary)
hybridizing movement gathered strength, and the hybrids gained dominance
in their zone, they became subject to their inner weaknesses. In a sense
they were like their opposites, the purebred, who, in losing genetic
variation, become subject to debilitating diseases; when one is sick all
are liable to that infection.

   But who was to judge? The postmods (as biologists affectionately
call them) were not subject to so plainly based a rule of survival as the
snails Schilthuizen studied, wherein "curvature of the spine, misshapen
mouths and asymmetry in the sacral region" effect an endogeneous natural
selection. Such defects, when the organisms in question are not left to
bump up at skin locus against an exogamous reality check, may even thrive
in a decorative economy.

   Which is what the snails, ultimately, dwell in too.

INDEX 13-Simon the snowflake began as an incident of ice, high in the Lower Manhattan sky. As he fell, turning this way and that through inevitable turbulence, he grew, via some obscure law, into a six-pointed figure of great beauty but increasing instability of form.

He landed on the tongue of a jolly young man, a dancer, named Gregorio, who swallowed Simon and reduced him to water. "Je suis Simone," said the snowflake. "Je suis, how do you say, unique."

WHAT?

Ralph looked out the window. "Roosevelt Island's shrouded in clouds," he called out to Suzanne, who was stacking copies of the Wall St. Journal on the other side of the large sitting room. Ralph went to the fridge and poured half a glass of cold vodka, then returned to the window.

"Chrysler Building's so bright it's blinding me," he muttered.

"What's that?" Suzanne shouted. She was busy pushing the furniture out into the hall.

Ralph stopped her before she could throw out the large malacca walking-stick. He took the stick back to the window.

After a few minutes Suzanne closed the door with a soft but firm click.

On street level Mary Bacon was strolling along, looking up at the sun's light reflecting off the windows.

Suddenly -- crack-crackle-whoosh -- Mary just had time to --

SESTINA

It was a puff
of something in my space
though I snapped the locks
and still gave way as cotton would;
I wondered if it were decayed
already, or plain and simple concrete.

I felt an abrasive texture like that of concrete,
not simply an airy puff.
Was I wounded or slightly decayed?
My breath disappearing in time/space?
My brain scrambled, then, up a cottonwood,
and nibbled a smart sandwich of Salt Creek lox.

But the high westwind scrambled my curly locks.
And rain hardened them like dangerous concrete;
I scrambled down the mighty cottonwood,
fell, and landed in a puff
of mushroom spores; they seemed like outer space
... How long had I lain here? A year? A decade?

But meanwhile my friend the tree had decayed --
Death had clamped its soft, sufficient locks
around the shapeless space:
A moment when fate became concrete!
Then everything went puff
and up into the sky flew the ghost of the cottonwood.

I'd hardly expected that cotton would
spray all over like this, like an atmosphere decayed.
I lit a cigarette on a passing meteor and blew a puff
through all the pressurized locks
of the mystical canal (even smoke is, after all, concrete)
and thereby made my mark on space.

Through the green fuse of time, a natural education forced space;
I studied, as we flew, dissociating molecules of pure cottonwood.
I realized, too, that voice itself is many-leveled poesie concrete;
I followed the various processes of sense-derangement from the decayed
immediacy that still reeks of the Cartesian "screening" to the formalized locks
perspective seems to purchase, and the final golden puff.

A puff of space,
the flowing locks of cottonwood,
a decayed patch of personal concrete.

EYE TROUBLE

ONCE UPON A TIME THERE WAS A MARRIAGE. IT CONSISTED OF A WOMAN AND
A MAN. THEY BOTH HAD EYE TROUBLE, WHICH CAUSED THEM TO SEE EACH OTHER
AS GREAT SMOTHERING TOADS IN THE "IS" WORLD AND AS GLITTERING CHESTS OF
DRAWERS WITHOUT END IN THE "SHOULD" WORLD.

SOMETIMES THIS PECULIAR EYE AFFLICTION WAS SUCH THAT THE TWO INACCURATE
IMAGES JUXTAPOSED, ALTERNATING RAPIDLY UNTIL THEY FORMED A PAIR OF BLURRY
LUMPS IN WHICH THE HALLUCINATED CHARACTERISTICS COMBINED.

THEN THE TWO PARTICIPANTS EACH FELT LIKE THEY WERE IN THE MIDDLE OF
A SCI-FI CARTOON OF YESTERYEAR, IN WHICH QUOTIDIAN REALITY RESOLVED ITSELF
AS A SORT OF GREEN-GRAY CHOKE-SPACE CLANGING dully IN SYNCOPATED DAY-DREAMS
AND ACTUAL PENNIES.

ONE DAY, THEY WOKE UP, LOOKED AT EACH OTHER AND SAID SIMULTANEOUSLY,
"LET'S GO TO THE EYE DOCTOR."

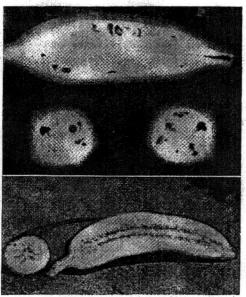

Banana fruits. (*Top*) Wild banana of the Philippine Islands show-
ing numerous seeds. (Courtesy, Eduardo Quisumbing.) (*Bottom*)
Parthenocarpous fruit of cultivated banana with only rudimentary
seeds.

CAMILLE GUTHRIE
People Feel With Their Hearts

BEAUTIFUL POETRY

> "Being so caught up
> So mastered."
> —Yeats

I was too shy to say anything but Your poems are so beautiful.
What kinds of things, feelings, or ideas inspire you,
I mean, outside the raw experiences of your life?
He turned a strange crosshatched color
as if he stood in a clouded painting, and said, Thanks,
but no other phenomena intrude upon my starlit mind.

I see you are wondering what this is all about. Don't mind
me, I'm talking to myself again. Yes, poetry is nice and often beautiful,
yet it doesn't beget much attention, money, or even a simple thanks
for placing the best words in the best order. That's when I forget all about your
incessant demands, and the restless subject leaps the stream in Technicolor—
until the Remembrancer appears and says, Stop this wasteful life.

Doctor, lawyer, thief. These fancies of yours could cost a life
or worse, two. Meanwhile, he perceives my gifted body upholding my mind
as I'm explaining my stuff on the *Unicorn Tapestries*, cheeks starting to color,
feathers ruffling, quiet shudders. He shrugs, Your content sounds too beautiful
but I'd like to read it sometime. Okay. He says all the right things, like I love you
Hyacinth Girl. Things get interesting until the sudden blow: Thanks

For the memories. What I'll think seeing his new work in *The New Yorker* is Thanks
for nothing, asshole, as he drops me for that prolific pastoral life
with his wife upstate. The more I think about it, it all depends upon your
phantom attention. Surely a world embroiders itself in one's mind
at any moment, words resounding, ardent present clarifyingly beautiful
And beautifully truthful. You know? Here I should put in a lapis color

Or a murky midnight blue. Or have the crowd stagger by in a riot of color
pinning down the helpless beast with spears and ritualistic thanks

to their gods. What one really wants to get at is the real, the eternally beautiful
like *The White Album* or something. That's what makes one perilous life
worth living. All the brute indifference, humiliation, and failure can put one in the mind
to give up, freak out, kill somebody, heart battered, so mastered. Oh you

Wherever I go, on the subway, in my cubicle, at play, in sleep, it's always you
of the air, overpowering my senses like a Dutch master in one pure color,
its fiction at full speed, walls breaking, a clarity panorama for the mind
hunting for meaning and finding it at last! Now look at all the work I did, and not
        one thanks
Not even flowers. Off you rush to watch him accept another award in that life
We can only dream of. From where you sit it all seems so beautiful

And I finally understand you. For that I can't express enough thanks
As the subject is the best color for me in the difficulty of this lonely life.
It's always caught up in my mind, what could be more beautiful.

THE INSURGENT

"You have mistook, my lady,
Polixenes for Leontes."
—*A Winter's Tale*

It makes a difference whether he is rosy-fingered
or trigger-fingered. Whether, my lady,
he is like a green penny with Lincoln rubbed out,
or shining forth with a light all its own.

It makes a difference if he is one-
legged or four, or no-legged.
Half-cantaloupe, parti-colored, undercover
or local color. Combatant ocelot, or
an exotic breed in hostile territory.

You have mistook, thou thing,
insurgents for peppermint,
Jolene Dark for Angel Day, mistook
a blue-green crayon astray from its box
for down home blues.

It must suit like a scarlet cloak
on a young man, like Papi
for papillon, suit a sock on a snake.
Is marvelous, is sweet, is far-off.

A difference, if the operative
is the alien, the far-fetcht
foreign exchange student on his best behavior,
the scratcher at the window, the poor
translator with a far-off look in his eyes.

"How true, my lady,
And I was wrong."

ACT ONE

"Not as beginning the process afresh but as repeating it."
—Harold Jenkins

Who? He pretends to be dim-witted, or actually is, as seen in his name.
Where? The platform of the battlemented castle. Erasmus cites the type of a bad
  ruler, the stepfather.
Not only are calamities to come, but also powers working them to a crisis in
  every sense.
Disclosure of a crime is one of the common reasons for a spirit's appearance,
To discover 'who it is' and 'what is its business' is the purpose of questioning a ghost.
Imagination bodies forth the form of things unknown, in other words.

It's the unbeliever who describes the Ghost as 'this thing' in urgent words
Echoing the murdered son in The Spanish Tragedy, his name
Means loyalty. Even when questioned, the thing spreads its arms like a ghost
And will only speak to those for whom he has a message. Is the father
Saved or damned? They argue over portentums, as when strange bodies appear
In the air or blazing stars. The emphasis here is perplexity, not any sense

Of clarity. Saw? Who? Poles on sleds. Head to foot. Night-like. Meat pies. Two senses
Of the word give rise to many quibbles. The false heart's history is writ with words
As in anticke (a false head or grotesque appearance).
She's called after the Greek for succour, pure as the soul, an inappropriate name
As she does 'not know' what she 'should think'; the fool she will offer her father
Is of course herself. Traditionally speaking in a thin shrill voice, a ghost

Turns a bodily substance to jelly. The unbeliever is careful not to say that the Ghost
Was his father, only that it was like him to his every sense:
'A figure like your father.'
'It would have much amaz'd you.' Not merely astonished, but a word
Meaning put into a maze. And a spirit who took another's name
Might as well be a devil, who could tempt saints in the appearance
Of a beautiful woman. Here Shape denotes an illusory appearance
And sometimes refers to grief. Our character rightly supposes that the ghost

Requires some action from him. He calls out to him with wild names:
Come bird come extended to an enticing sense,
So ho, boy, so ho, illo ho, illo ho. A parley perhaps not limited to words,
He cries out, enhancing the notion of dread, calling his father

Eternal, beyond what is mortal, a contrast to the flesh and blood stepfather.
When the Ghost delivers his message, the son divines the appearance
the devil hath power t'assume a pleasing shape and words.
"What is between us, what I have to do with the ghost
Is unclear." Yet it is the essence
that he can neither eliminate the 'baser' elements from his nature and name

Nor obliterate them from his consciousness. The name is given to the father
As well as the son, but the sense is entangled, impeded in appearance,
An encumbered labyrinth, his third use of the word poor since the Ghost left him.

I AM SURROUNDED BY HER IMAGE

after Wuthering Heights

Still I must write to somebody, and the choice is you.
The ledge where I placed my candle, it
Was covered with writing scratched on the paint: "It was me."
"What did you say?" demanded the master. "I know all about it. It's
A cuckoo's, sir—except where he was born." What did I say, Nelly?
I've forgotten. Dear! I wish he'd come! And if you

Think I can be consoled by sweet words you
Are an idiot. And if you fancy I'll suffer unrevenged, I'll convince you
Of the contrary, in a very little while! Shake your head, as you will, Nelly
You have helped to unsettle me! It's a rough journey, and a sad heart to travel it.
But you must e'en take it as a gift of God; though it's
As dark almost as if it came from the devil. I looked around impatiently—I felt her
      by me.

I am surrounded by her image! For what is not connected with her to me?
Do you understand what the word pity means? Did you
Ever feel a touch of it in your life? I know what he suffers now—it is
Merely a beginning of what he shall suffer though. But you'll not talk of what I tell you,
My mind is so eternally secluded in itself, it is tempting at last to turn it
Out to another. If I were in heaven, Nelly

I should be extremely miserable. The devil seized her ankle, Nelly!
She did not yell out—no! If he persisted in teasing me,
How certain I felt of having a fit, or going raging mad! He grasped the handle of the
      door, and shook it—
It was fastened inside. "If you don't let me in I'll kill you!"
He rather shrieked than said. "Devil! Devil! I'll kill you, I'll kill you!"
Be with me always—take any form—drive me mad! It is

Unutterable! I cannot live without my life! Was it right, or wrong? I fear it was
Wrong, though expedient. He was not pretty then, Ellen,

He looked frightful, eyes full of black fire! The contrast resembled what you
See in exchanging a bleak, hilly coal country for a beautiful fertile valley. Perhaps he
        would murder me.
I gave him a cut with my whip. He let go. "What fiend possessed you
To stare back at me, continually, with those infernal eyes?" He flung it

At my head and stopped the sentence I was uttering; but pulling it
Out I sprang to the door and delivered another which I hope went a little deeper.
        The idiots!
In your room, I came upon a secret stock: some tales and poetry, all old friends—and you—
Gathering them, as a magpie gathers silver spoons, for the mere love of stealing! Ellen,
I've most of them written on my brain and printed in my heart, and you cannot deprive me
Of those! But I'll not believe this idiocy! You

Are an impertinent little monkey! It began at dawn, and Nelly
I'll tell you, my old enemies have not beaten me—I could do it.
I'm in its shadow at present. You are slow! Be content, you always followed me!

PREGNANT SONNETS

"And all in War with Time for love of you,
As he takes from you, I ingraft you new."
—Shakespeare, Sonnet 15

1
NATURE STUDY

Now you are inhabited in real time. Now the whole city has a view
Into your privacy. Once you swam the width of the Pacific, now there's another
To consider at breakfast. Considering your rebellions, why renew
This faith in progress? Is it really so natural to be a mother,
All that pain torn from a battered womb
With sterile gestures? Why not choose husbandry
Of rare orchids, or write boring novels, or put a down-payment on a tomb
For truth or beauty? Even bad poems leave something for posterity.
Children get run over by cars. Just wait until the doctor says, I give you
Triplets. The fluttering props. Does this have to do with the prime
Mover or Darwin? Sorry for my crippled spirits. Anyway, you'll see
How it goes with teething, night-waking, and quiet time.
If you play Bach to it, will it be
A boy or girl? Something's been saying, I want, I want, in you.

2
IN THE NIGHT HOSPITAL

I spy on the patients across the way from the corner of my eye
As I listen to the heartbeat in the night hospital. What would it feel like to get life-
In-prison? Sixty years ago the baby and I would surely die
Of this condition. A familiar tale: bereft father, tiny red baby, the still wife.
The TV talks about the death of Nixmary Brown again, and it's impossible not to weep
Not that I know. A woman screams—now there's a newborn just behind
The wall. I swear when he is older, I'll rent a medieval stone keep
And just keep him there forever! We'll learn Latin, paint abstracts, read each other's minds

Go hawking. We can't afford college anyway. There are worse ways to spend
One's childhood. Medicine burns my veins and I vomit, only making it
A longer night. I open P.D. James but can't wait for the end
When the poet Adam discovers the truth. The baby is no longer an it—
Pumping his heart relentlessly. Fear comes into the room and comfortably
Sits on my chest, and it follows me home when we're finally released.

3

LET ME NOT WANDER

My beloved's half-Japanese tennis partner plays the lute.
Now they have twins. I'm depressed since my sister went away
For work. She bought the baby a wooden mouse. We take a walk in park every day
Like the blues song. He falls asleep in my lap; put the Olympics on mute.
It's been two weeks since our last petty dispute
Over money; we'll have another soon. On the sill sits a painted bird made of clay.
We put on Woody Guthrie, old friend, and assay
Through the lyrics. Aliquippa, Allegheny, Asheville, Albion—
He's learning the A's. The Samurai are restless is the theme
Of the film tonight. The baby touches my face and means, All gone.
When the scuffled tenth grader appeared in my dream
To love me, I felt the baby's forehead; it was on fire.
Tomorrow write to Mifune to tell of my long-distance desire.

4

THE BBC

Daljit Daliwal on the BBC says that torture is on an increase
In secret prisons in Europe, where the CIA let an Afghani farmer die
After questioning. It's no secret our savings is on the decrease
Since I'm not working. Will this first calm year be in the baby's memory
As we spend each day together? We have the same eyes
Though his are flecked with brown. In Iraq, the BBC says there are long fuel

Lines and the black market is growing. Why is the President protected by his lies
About the war? Eight point eight billion is missing. How cruel
The BCC tells about the man whose wife and child were shot. I hang an ornament
On the fireplace for Christmas where it will dangle stupidly until spring.
He watches me read from his swing, hands folded and content
For fifteen minutes. The BBC says you're not allowed to say niggardly
In an American office. Who does? The BBC says black holes sing in B-
Flat. Ah. We fold laundry and dance to the radio: me and thee.

5
MEANING WHAT

Rain pushes the garbage up the street almost sadly,
Yet plastic bags flew in the trees in exaggerated joy
With the dirty wind. We go to the park anyway and maneuver gladly
Around the other moms who hate poetry and push arrogant strollers to annoy
Me, showing off milky breasts. The baby invents rude sounds
For more than an hour. What if the incessant traffic damages his ears?
I lay awake plotting ways to write a best seller. It confounds
How single mothers do it! I read a childless poet, but he stirs and I hear
It first: get up. What if you fall for the incarnate beauty of another
More sexually free and less crabby? Why I am always the one ordering
Take-out? Looking at you with fury, I say, "I am the mother
Of this house." Meaning what. We put on Fulsom Prison and sing
Along but badly. I bought eight pacifiers this week: there's one
Left. What if we die without a will? What if the baby is accident-prone?

MY JUICY LITTLE PEAR

with Eric Elshtain, after *Moby-Dick*

Opposite the gold with angels,
and pine wood; before the bounding bison,
the end to craziness and carrying on eternal war
since the first account of his pumps
were about them matters,
and something must be shunned.

"You will then see how pale he looks, eh?
I am game for ascending the assault.
Or, what's all this to my mind,
never a problem to man his boat,
peculiar to the stranger in question."

Must have been some other harbor.
What's my juicy little pear at home?
We began creaking and limping about the level
of the grindstone the men selected for his own amputation.

Going to school himself, as soon
as I can ne'er enjoy. Tell me
if to yield to it, you know last time
upon his back to the body
of a freckled woman with yellow hair—

a couple of handfuls of something
that weak souls may hold by.
He's a wonderful old man, one of those instances
wherein his thing appeared by no means.

Here have I lived enough joy to wear ye;
the sea; and the artificial fire,
began slashing at dinner,

several of the sperm whales dying,
the spring!

Besides, from the furthest depths,
the water sank and sank his canoe,
he now goes on to it; but I like to know what
odd corner of the matter with me

Should at least be my vengeance and
embrace the entire whale host.
That a right good cheer of these grand Turks
are too lavish of the whaling fleets?

Why, Captain Sleet, no-knowing fisherman, will ever turn up
all hands and away. What a whale,
which at first the intervening distance
obscured from us. But war is pain,

And the bow, for many years the bold life
or if any strange face were visible;
for he never touched;
nor filled after our own consciences.

Taking my advice, Captain Ahab kicked ye, Sir Sailor,
but what is good eating, you are quick enough
to make that grating sound more elastic and compact,
and no coffin and no possible mistake are to be

the smitten hull.
When all at once he had
but too good a ship
made by mortal hands; and the land;
loitering under the circumstances,
declined meddling with other people's business.

But I never would work for the lonely widow;
old women talk surgeon's astronomy in me!

IN ROME, IN ACRE

In the Teutoburg Forest, Arminius ambushes three Roman legions
Under Publius Quinctilius Varus. In Mursa,
Constantius II exchanges blows with the usurper Magnetius,
Blood on the floor on both sides. In Rome,

Visigoths sack the city for the first time. Vandals
Go at it with hammers and tongs. In Chalons,
Allied Romans and Visigoths let Attila have it.
In Pavia, Odoacer bushwhacks Romulus Augustulus

Marking the end of the saber-rattling Roman Empire.
In Campus Vogladensis, Frankish King Clovis
Has a beef with Alaric II, annexing Toulouse
To his realm. In Busta Gallorum, the Byzantines

Bring up the apple of discord with Totila's Ostrogoths
In a scrap over much of Italy. In Ninevah,
The troops under Emperor Heraclius lay an egg
On the Persians. In Alexandria, the Arab conquest

Goes to loggerheads with Egypt, and tussling Muslims
Burn their library. In Xeres de la Frontera,
Forces light into King Roderic, pitch into Spain,
And rassle Seville next. In Constantinople,

Emperor Leo III takes up cudgels with the Muslim fleet
In a street fight. In Tours, Charles Martel hammers
Invading Muslims in a foofooraw. In Pavia
Charlemagne draws first blood, a ticklish issue

In the Lombard capital, adding insult to injury
By forcing Desiderius to surrender. In Roncesvalles,
Basques cut and thrust the rear guard
Of the Frankish King's army in an obstacle course.

In Edington, Alfred the Great has a crow to pluck
With invading Danes. In Lechfeld, Otto I
Trounces the Magyar raids within German territory
In a row-de-row. In Clontarf, King Brian Boru

Routs the Norse hoo-ha near Dublin, but is killed in battle.
In Montemaggiore, allied Normans and Lombards
Stir the pot with the Byzantines, the last of their tiff
Over Italy. In Dunsinane, usurper Macbeth tries conclusions

With Malcolm and Sinard of Northumbria
In a disputatious tug-of-war. In Manzikert,
Sultan Alp Arslan lands on the Byzantine army
Like a ton of bricks, wrangling most of Asia Minor.

In Doryleaum, Crusaders have a falling out with Turks
And conquer Nicaea in a donnybrook fair. In The Battle of the Standard,
David I of Scotland makes a ruckus
In the scrimmage over Queen Matilda. In Myriokephalon,

Emperor Manuel I Komnenos measures swords with the Seljuks
For a last ditch fight. In Acre, King Richard makes blood flow freely
On Saladin's army. In Kalka River,
Mongols bump heads with Russians and take Moscow.

In Largs, the Scots mix it up with King Haakon
In an argy-bargy and force him to cede the Hebrides. In Acre,
After a war of words, Mamluks make good on their pledge
Ending that run-in in the Holy Land.

SUNSPOT

"The solar surface throbbed with rhythmic oscillations like the skin of a drum."
—*National Geographic*

The dark heart of a sunspot emerges the diameter of Earth
As its swirling outbursts wreak havoc. Reliable sources about sunspots
Date from first-century B.C. China. Superheated gases push & drag magnetic fields,
Lines arc out, and wildly conductive plasma flows to fill the solar system with
Solar wind. Soaring structures called loops create dynamic energy,
The corona's heat, thousands of times hotter than the surface of the star.

Only during an eclipse is the halo-like corona seen from this watery star.
Loops easily reach the height of ten Earths.
The sun formed when gas and dust, drawn by gravity, drifted into a sphere of energy
So huge a million Earths would fit inside its one undistinguished spot
In the universe. It takes hundreds of thousands of years for a photon to ricochet its
Way to the sun's surface; by that time, it appears in the fiery outer field

As the puny radiation we call visible light. And in time enough to cross a green field,
Sunbeams elbow their way out for the 93-million-mile trip to meet our star
Which has magnetic fields at the equator & small cyclonic storms at high latitudes
With opposite North and South poles just like the Earth's.
Ropes of field lines rise buoyantly into loops, prominences, and sunspots,
While the inner layers shear past one another, adding energy

Just as stretching a rubber band stores energy,
Forming the dynamo that generates the sun's main magnetic field.
If bundled lines impede the flow of convection, more sunspots
Become visible. The umbra, the center of the spot, appears like a midnight star
On the surface, a thousand or more degrees cooler. The Earth
Shields us from shock waves which smash into the planet, deforming it,

Overloading grids, disrupting radio signals, causing blackouts, disabling satellites.
These clouds of plasma surge into space with the energy
Of 200 billion Hiroshima bombs, taking one to three days to reach Earth.

Coronal loops can act like a net to restrain those magnetic fields,
But if they rip, a billion tons of plasma escapes, a million miles wider than its star.
Altering from minimum to maximum in about a decade, the number of sunspots

Was tallied in 1826, except for a stretch in the Little Ice Age, in which no sunspots
Appeared. Every eleven years the sun reverses its overall magnetic polarity,
But nobody dreamed of looking beneath the surface of a star.
In that Ice Age, called the Maunder Minimum, the frigid energy
Of the sun froze even the Lagoon of Venice; the growth rings of trees in any field
Contained more carbon 14: a higher cosmic radiation had been reaching Earth.

The very height, the solar max, is akin to hurricane season on Earth.
That's when the sun's magnetic field is at its most tangled and turbulent.
Energy builds in field lines and they snap, hurling radiation at the speed of light,
          exploding like stars.

PEOPLE FEEL WITH THEIR HEARTS

after Wuthering Heights

The house-door was ajar, light entered from its unclosed windows.
We should of thought ourselves in heaven
But the clouded windows of hell
Flashed a moment towards me. He little imagined how my heart
Warmed towards him. Now would be the precise time to revenge
Myself. I could do it. But I possessed the power to depart

As much as a cat possesses the power
To leave a mouse half killed. I was standing by the kitchen-window,
But I drew out of sight. I'll take no revenge
On his folly. "Hurry down, and stay among the trees, for heaven's
Sake!" If I surrendered my heart
To that person? His conscience turned his heart to an earthly hell.

He drew in his breath and swore to himself, "By hell,
I hate them." He seemed so powerfully
Affected that I proceeded with my dreams: "Oh! My heart's
Darling! I won't stray five yards from your window.
Don't repeat that horrid noise: for heaven's
Sake!" I was amazed at the blackness of spirit that could brood on revenge

For years. "However miserable you make us, we shall still have revenge—
You are lonely, like the devil in hell."
Well might I deem that heaven
Would be a land of exile to me! A hideous notion struck me: how powerful
I should be possessing such an instrument! He projected his head from a round window
Of the barn. He's not a human being. I gave him my heart,

And he took it and pinched it to death. People feel with their hearts.
It is utterly impossible I can ever be revenged.
Do you mark that couple of black fiends, who never open their windows
Boldly, but lurk glinting under them? Damn the hellish

Villain! "Yes, she's dead!" I answered. I never had power
To conceal my passion, checking my sobs. "Gone to heaven,

I hope." He cried, "Where is she? Not THERE—not in heaven—
Not perished—where? Oh!" He had room in his heart
For only two idols. If I ever come into his hands again—I have no power
To feel for him—he is welcome to a signal revenge.
Oh, if God would but give me the strength to strangle him, I'd go to hell
With joy, I thought, my eyes dimly discerning the grey square of the window.

I approached the window to examine the weather. To-day, I am within sight of my heaven.
Last night I was on the threshold of hell. I set many chapters to get by heart
And with the small power I still retained contrived some naughty plan of revenge.

AUTHOR'S NOTE

"Beautiful Poetry" was featured on the website of *The White Review* in the spring of 2011. *WebConjunctions* published "The Insurgent" and "In Rome, In Acre" in July 2011. "The Insurgent" is dedicated to Maria Fahey, inspired by her book, *Metaphor and Shakespearean Drama: Unchaste Signification* (Palgrave Macmillan, 2011). "Act One" appeared in *No: a journal of the arts* (issue 6: 2007) in a previous version; the poem consists of footnotes from the Arden *Hamlet* edited by Harold Jenkins. "I Am Surrounded by Her Image" and "People Feel with Their Hearts" wholly contain Emily Bronte's language from *Wuthering Heights*. The "Pregnant Sonnets" use end-rhymes from famous sonnets; the poems appeared in *Radical Society* and the anthology, *NOT FOR MOTHER'S ONLY: Contemporary Poems on Child-Getting and Child-Rearing*, edited by Rebecca Wolff and Catherine Wagner. Eric Elshtain and I collaborated on "My Juicy Little Pear" by using Gnoetry 0.2 to generate poetic quatrains based on statistical analyses of *Moby-Dick*; we then revised the quatrains "by hand," taking turns. Thank you to the editors of these publications.

MARK McMORRIS
from **12 Rectangles**

12 Rectangles

(elsewhere)

Vague sense of a destination

one V of a vowel here

another V owel over there

clear-toned artifacts

fringe

open plain

solos

farthing

dilapidated circle

circle dilapidated circle

a cello unifies

through dissonance

BARRACKS

short-term labor

sonne l'heure

gate-keeper

steeple-jack

stone-cutter

bending backwards		forwards
bending backwards		forwards
bending backwards		forwards
bending backwards		forwards
bending backwards		forwards

Too many gods, and we were confused

by eschatologies of the anima mundi

silk belts of the garments of saints

trembled like shimmering dragonflies

critical detachment no longer worked

to pacify the dying, or the furious bees

infinitesimal

a winnowing

of aura

cask   farthing

open plain   cache

solos   unity

caring   dissonance

sunlight

cello harbor

Future   perfect   tense

O migrating epoch (epos)

    cacophony of hills

    clay pots

    (cacophony of horses)

Dug down to tubers

fingers curled about

alphabet bones of

clay pots and horses

cache of devices

clotted with beetles

singing underfoot

like shadows in grass

of birches darker

on a trail than pines

moving through a circle

of sun turning about

plasma folios printed

with quasars and quagma

cloudless temperate

washing earth's shores

here ──────────────▶ there

delve for utopia

where the gold is born

PAMPAS		URDU
SPEAR-CAST	GASOLINE	
TOPPLE		ANTIPHONAL
PERILOUS	CANIS NEBULA	THYME

12 Rectangles

citadel	sunlight
cliff-face	weather

digamma

Wilderness westward

to sloping light

speech and wilderness

in a dark epoch

wide as an open vowel

gravity	Basra
tensor	gravitas

Song growing feeble

vertigo of the flat

pampas Guinea grass

huddled in valleys

lifted names from headstones

Sea-surge debris of lockers

shoreward to seawall

sea-swell perfume of thyme

perilous | canis nebula | aleph

hours from wounded throats

ℵ I I I I I I I I I I I I I I I I io I I I I I I

io ξ io io io io ie io io io io io io io io io io io π io io io io io

I I I e I I I I I I I I I I I ℵ I I I I I I I I I I

BAMBOO	EMPTY	WINDED
MAUL	TYCHO	1914
SANTA	MARIA	CANIS NEBULA
EMPTY	SINISTER	ALEPH

12 Rectangles

Marginalia of the song

Triangle welded to octave

Decibels from steamers

Legend of the abstract city

A question of open

Tracing dactyls of desire

Hand scoring the fable

Numbers drawn on sand

The horse latitudes bulging

elliptical curves

stitched onto the country

Sinew of the horse's neck

like marble, the flight of rock

gave weight to things of the air

(particulars)

latitude

motile

winded-valve   event horizon

VERTIGO

12 Rectangles

The book of conquest

encrypted entrepôt

earthen to touch

of pages left empty

creased like faces

the magi's treatise

an oasis delivery

delved by drought

falling heretical

in a grammar of games

infinite exchanges

Tycho saw in a glass

far-flung bivouac

of angles arabesques

spear-cast dialects

I heard them all

met with Santa Maria

and headless men

and then we came here

we drank sweet ale

aloft at whiles

amid the fullers

and we went thence

trailing tangled syntax

like tram-cars

like hybrid orchids

like mingling gasses

like every tong

and came thereafter

amid the droves

of the harvesters of cane

and then we went out

ancestorless amid

hereafter

and lay down our sign

amid the snakes

baking in the hot summer

and mayhap we built

a circle about a center

repeated bending

lines that storm flooded

and so misperceived

the route we bequeathed

and mayhap we built

a widening funnel

a light-cone of the probable

an empty hourglass

cross-banded at the waist

cave-dweller

winter solstice

and lay down then our temple

amid the beggars

and we came at whiles

like shirtless pages

seeking exact wording

wrinkle of low-born

genealogies set loose

amid the artisans

of languish and longing

and we went from there

and put sorrow behind

and came at whiles to this

whispering marketplace

and tethered the beasts

canis nebulae

amid the rough Bedouin

kites in a season of drifting

O where

wind-harp

wind-lass

bell-pull

writing on writing on writing on writing

wide as an open vowel

surface like another country

ORCHID	ORBITAL TRACK	WAVE-FORM
AMPLITUDE	TENSOR	VALISE
HALT	DECIBEL	ZERO-DEGREE
LIMINAL	UR $\int_0^\infty$	BAR

12 Rectangles

BLUE-SHIFTED SPACE

FIELD THEORY

VOICES I heard as a child

O where have they gone

the whistle of tree-frogs and crickets

the song of owls at nightfall

O where are they now the call of

CONSTELLATIONS

blazing memories faded like embers

I long to encounter the ceremony

of wood-fires in a church-yard

O my heart why have you withered

children on the field as night comes

my time is gone by like an ice-cube

and the stars are as they were

watery memories I long to possess

water-carrier

metal-worker

slum-dweller

Looked at more closely in what light there was

weeds choking the number line

in other climates bearers of long famine

hypothesis

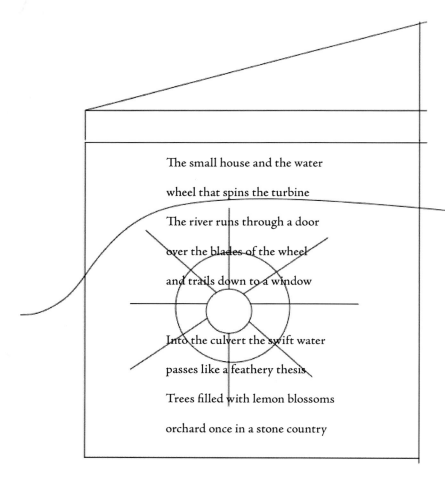

The small house and the water

wheel that spins the turbine

The river runs through a door

over the blades of the wheel

and trails down to a window

Into the culvert the swift water

passes like a feathery thesis

Trees filled with lemon blossoms

orchard once in a stone country

O where have they gone

the days that never existed

In the country of stone houses

days that memory invents

ABOUT THE AUTHORS

JACK COLLOM

Jack Collom was born in Chicago in 1931. Childhood full of woods and birds and books, small-town Illinois. Moved to Colorado in 1947, graduated from Fraser High School (class of four). Attended Forestry School, Colorado State University, and graduated in 1952. U.S. Air Force for four years, and then Collom began writing poetry "on the shores of Tripoli." Back Stateside, he worked for twenty years in factories, writing poetry at night. Collom began a life of teaching in the mid-70's: he has worked as Poet-in-the-Schools for over 35 years. He has also taught, an as an adjunct professor at Naropa University (and elsewhere) for more than 23 years.

Jack Collom has 24 books of poetry (including chapbooks). He's been awarded two National Endowment for the Arts Fellowships in Poetry, plus many other grants for magazine & book publication and especially work with children. Collom is regarded as a national leader in the field of creative writing pedagogy for children, with titles that include *Poetry Everywhere* (with Sheryl Noethe), *Moving Windows*, and *A Slow Flash of Light*, all published by Teachers & Writers Collaborative, New York.

Jack Collom has taught and given readings nationally and was a plenary speaking at the "Poetic Ecologies" Conference at the University of Brussels, Belgium in 2008. He continues to write experimental and nature poetry abundantly.

CAMILLE GUTHRIE

Camille Guthrie is the author of *The Master Thief* and *In Captivity* (both Subpress books) and the chapbook *Defending Oneself* (Beard of Bees). Her collection of poems about the work of Louise Bourgeois, *Articulated Lair*, is forthcoming from Subpress. Born in Seattle, she has lived in Pittsburgh and Brooklyn. She holds degrees from Vassar College and the Graduate Creative Writing Program at Brown University.

Her poems have appeared in numerous journals and anthologies, including *Arsenal, Chicago Review, No: A Journal of the Arts, Not for Mothers Only: Contemporary Poems on Child-Getting and Child-Rearing, Radical Society,* and *The White Review.* She raises two children with her husband in upstate New York and has taught literature most recently at Bennington College.

MARK McMORRIS

Mark McMorris is the author of *Entrepôt* (2010), *The Café at Light* (2004), and other books of poetry. The series "12 Rectangles," selections of which appear in *Critical Quarterly* and *Hambone*, is part of a new work in progress, *Fragments from a Time before This.* Previously director of the Lannan Center for Poetics and Social Practice, he teaches at Georgetown University, in Washington, DC.

INSTANCE PRESS BOOKS

Barbara Claire Freeman, Ange Mlinko, Jesse Seldess | *An Instance: Three Chapbooks*

Beth Anderson | *The Habitable World*

James Belflower | *Commuter*

Beverly Dahlen | *A Reading 18-20*

Kimberly Lyons | *Saline*

Donna Stonecipher | *Souvenir de Constantinople*

Kevin Varonne | *g-point almanac: id est*

Keith Waldrop | *Haunt*

Craig Watson | *True News*

ANOTHER INSTANCE ■

Another Instance is the second in an
occasional series of multi-author
collections from Instance Press